THE ARCHER AND ANNA HYATT HUNTINGTON
SCULPTURE GARDEN

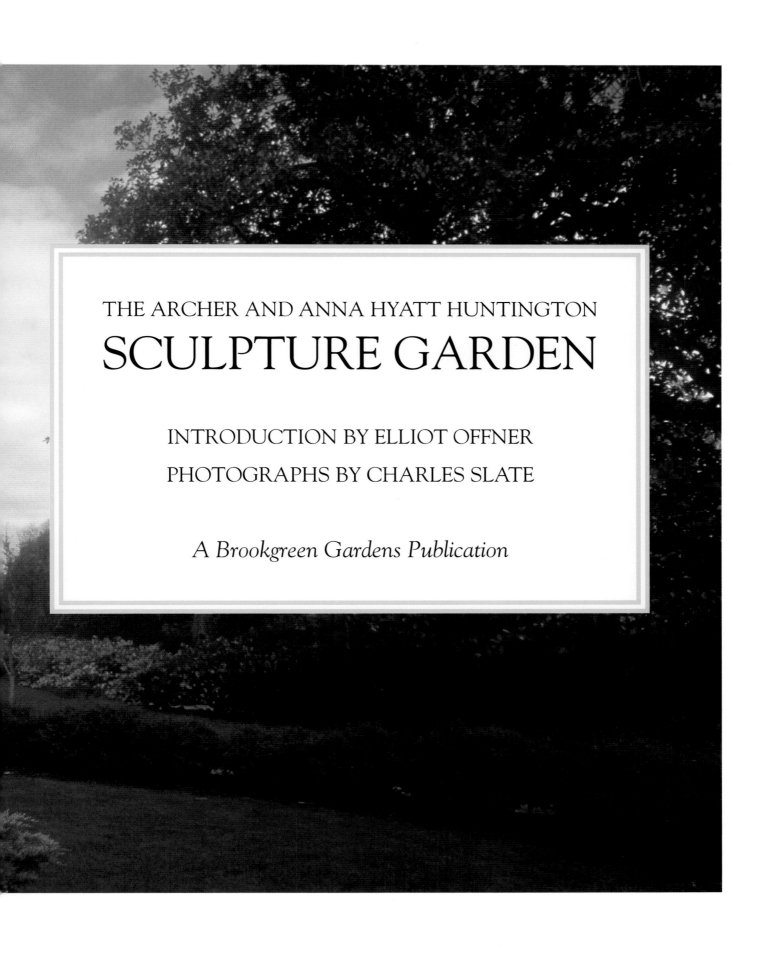

THE ARCHER AND ANNA HYATT HUNTINGTON
SCULPTURE GARDEN

INTRODUCTION BY ELLIOT OFFNER

PHOTOGRAPHS BY CHARLES SLATE

A Brookgreen Gardens Publication

Published for Brookgreen Gardens by
Wyrick & Company
Post Office Box 89
Charleston, South Carolina 29402

Designed by Sally Heineman
Printed and bound in China

ISBN 0-941711-65-X

Title page: *Dionysus* - Edward McCartan

Contents

Preface

In October 2001, the Board of Trustees of Brookgreen Gardens officially named the garden rooms begun by the institution's founders as the Archer and Anna Hyatt Huntington Sculpture Garden. By so doing, the trustees extended to that remarkable couple the recognition for their founding gift now provided to other donors whose gifts, while less monumental, significantly enhance the institution.

As well, this action by the trustees identified the Huntington Sculpture Garden as one of the three principal components that now comprise Brookgreen Gardens. The other components are the Lowcountry History and Wildlife Preserve, an effort to conserve and to interpret for the public the distinctive landscapes, plants, animals and cultures of the South Carolina Lowcountry; and the Center for American Sculpture, a national artistic and research initiative devoted to figurative sculpture.

This book, the first since the naming of the sculpture garden, presents the consequence and the beauty of the Archer and Anna Hyatt Huntington Sculpture Garden in the words of Elliot Offner and the photography of Charles Slate. We thank them and the generations of artists, horticulturists, trustees, donors, employees and volunteers whose devoted efforts during the past seventy years have sustained and enhanced the Huntingtons' vision for Brookgreen Gardens.

Lawrence Henry
President
Brookgreen Gardens

Introduction

Writing a few pages about a collection of sculptures which is judged by connoisseurs and scholars to be the finest collection of American figurative art in existence is a privilege, an honor and a conundrum. It is a privilege and an honor to be asked to write about an institution which contains so many treasures. It is a conundrum because hundreds of these sculptures ask to be mentioned and described and given their place in any discussion about the Archer and Anna Hyatt Huntington Sculpture Garden at Brookgreen Gardens. If we mention the breathtaking *Iris* by Carl Paul Jennewein, dare we not acknowledge so many other important sculptures?

This is an impossible task not to offend the living and the dead, and to all, I apologize, as the limitations of space and the scope of my mission are conspirators against a fair tribute to every sculptor who has contributed to the magnificence of the Brookgreen treasure house. My goal is simply to give an artist's impression of this remarkable establishment. I am a user of the collection, a sculptor and a student most of my life, who studies what other figurative artists have done, how they have rendered form and what they have to say. Nowhere is the opportunity greater to see what American figurative sculptors of the last two hundred years have achieved, what they have said, and what meaning lies within their work than in the artworks represented here.

To help me in my mission, I began to study more rigorously the individual sculptures, not simply those which had the most appeal to me, but also those to which I was originally less responsive. I read all the material I could find, much of which was given to me by the curator of the collection, Robin Salmon. Her knowledge of the sculptors and the works of art at Brookgreen Gardens is minutely detailed and generously shared.

Brookgreen Gardens stands alone as the creation of two extraordinary minds and talents who brought into being this special place in a manner unknown anywhere else in the world. While the care and continued development of Brookgreen are the responsibility of the present and future overseers, its path was outlined and physically developed by the complementary geniuses, the great sculptor Anna Hyatt Huntington and her husband, the scholar, bibliophile, philanthropist and founder of museums, Archer Milton Huntington.

Gardens, of course, have been a passion of the civilized world since the beginning of recorded time. Each country, each culture and subculture has cultivated everything from patches of land to vast tracts of formal plantings, often as part of grand architectural settings. In the United States, there are over 450 large aboreta and botanical facilities where nature has been controlled and refined for the purposes of science, learning and aesthetic value. Gardens are places of the spirit, where the wonders of life reveal themselves in the infinite vocabulary of the forms and colors of things that grow and change. In 1930, when Archer and Anna Huntington bought Brookgreen Plantation and the contiguous three rice plantations that were to become Brookgreen Gardens, they were purchasing a place where the climate would be favorable to Anna's continuing recovery from tuberculosis, and where wildlife, old gardens, and ancient oak trees all lived together in regal splendor. Soon, Anna had made a drawing of a plan to serve as the basis for the new Brookgreen Gardens, as it would be named, incorporating remnants of the original Brookgreen Plantation garden and creating a new and beautiful adaptation of the land for walkways and places of contemplation. Her butterfly-shaped design would soon be fitted with new as well as old plantings, a heroic effort aimed at embellishing the considerable natural beauty of the region.

Early on, the Huntingtons realized that this site, as they were developing it, would serve brilliantly for the harmonious exhibition and integration of sculpture. While the idea of sculpture exhibited within a landscaped garden site was not unique—one thinks of the Boboli Gardens in Florence as well as earlier Roman sites—the vigor, zeal, and vision of the Huntingtons resulted in the building of an outdoor museum which was the first public sculpture garden in America. At the heart of the collection was the sculpture of Anna Hyatt Huntington, and the artistic beliefs of both Anna and Archer Huntington. She was a figurative artist, easily the greatest of the American animaliers, and surely in the first rank of the finest sculptors this country has produced.

Archer Huntington described his wife and himself decisively as classicists. This was a significant pronouncement for their patronage and for Brookgreen's future, for by the 1930s, new lines of thinking had shown themselves in the world of sculpture. By 1920, Constantin Brancusi had created one of his early, famous bird sculptures, a highly polished thin vertical bronze image surging upward, stripped of all unnecessary appendage. It was pure form, "seeking to capture the essence of flight." In the 1920s, Julio Gonzalez had begun to work in wrought iron and steel, using fire and welding as the vehicles for his sculptures. By the end of World War II, the welding torch would be a tool in the hands of most sculpture students across America. In the 1930s, Alexander Calder, the son of sculptor Stirling Calder, who is represented in the Brookgreen collection, was already creating works in wire and adding a revolutionary sculptural element: physical movement. The slightest wind would change the configuration of his delicately suspended steel shapes. These currents are but a few of the new ideas which were beginning to percolate in universities, art schools and museums across the country.

Form for its own sake, new materials, and the relentless pursuit of seemingly new ideas occupied a large part of the cultural landscape. In this cli-

mate, the Huntingtons chose another course as they moved ahead to acquire the work of sculptors whose art was dedicated to the representation of the human figure, and the animal and natural world. While we might question the nature of their decision, this commitment permitted a collection to become manifest which has no parallel and brooks no comparison from institutions where figurative sculpture is represented. The Huntingtons set out to collect the sculpture of the finest figurative artists working in America from whom they hoped to purchase the best examples of their work. As sculptures were acquired, the larger ones were sited in the garden in a manner that enhanced their beauty. The construction of elegant architectural sites and the accompanying landscaping for each sculpture are fundamental to the ideals of display at Brookgreen. In this aspect of the breadth and display of the collection, Brookgreen's achievement transcends anything I have seen in America or Europe. The formation of the collection began during a period when garden sculpture was an important element in the domestic landscape. Coupled with Archer Huntington's interest in history and the classical world, and Anna Hyatt Huntington's devotion to creatures and figures of the natural world, their course was preordained.

At the entrance to Brookgreen Gardens, Anna's over life-size *Fighting Stallions* is set at a high elevation. The silhouettes of these miraculous beasts are handsome from every angle. Huntington was well aware of the different configurations of the changing negative spaces between the horses as the viewer moves around the sculpture. The horses are cast in aluminum, a dull gray metal, which she was the first to use as it became a legitimate alternative to bronze. She was unwilling to be trapped by the traditions of bronze, which, for all its beauty, oxidizes over time in ways that are beyond the sculptor's control. Furthermore, the consensus among conservators that outdoor bronzes should be waxed at least once a year means that the surfaces reflect light, making the form visually hard to grasp. Anna believed that aluminum permitted a rendered form to be read and understood in any light. With no sheen, it reflected less light than bronze, and the textures which she often incorporated seemed to work harmoniously with her subtly modeled shapes. Her fighting stallions reveal her masterful grasp of anatomy, and demonstrate her ability to achieve an astonishing level of action and contained motion in her work. Each of the eight legs moves in a different way, as do the manes, tails and heads, attaining a precarious, even dizzying balance. It is a work of high design and masterful form, an introduction to both the collection of sculpture within the gardens and to the oeuvre of one of the nation's outstanding sculptors.

Proceeding along the entrance drive into Brookgreen Gardens, one passes the first internal figure, a bronze heroic sculpture by Donald de Lue, originally created as a memorial to American soldiers lost in combat at Omaha Beach in Normandy. Continuing, one encounters another sculpture created as a memorial—a large stone work by Anna called *Youth Taming the Wild*, a horse with a figure alongside. The Huntingtons decided that the large numbers of bronzes that would populate the garden needed a complementary medium—stone. Consequently, there are a number of carved works in a variety of stones, including marbles from Tennessee to Italy, Georgia pink, and ordinary limestone. I do not know of another place where one can see so many sculptures carved in different stones. An odd work, but a favorite of mine, is Eugenie Frederica Shonnard's grey marble *Marabou*. Shonnard is one of the many women sculptors represented at Brookgreen. I doubt that any other sculpture collection contains the work of so many women artists.

Further along the entrance drive, one sees on the right a beautifully modeled woman with upraised arms in a diaphanous flowing gown, seemingly walking into the water with long regal steps. She is *Wind on the Water* by Richard McDermott Miller, a leading figurative sculptor today. On the left is the entrance to the Huntington Sculpture Garden. Prominently displayed in the gardens are several works by Paul Manship, in which Manship exhibits the style of

modernity that we associate with him as well as the hearkening back to the sculptural vocabulary of other eras. His modeling of plants and hair remind us of the ancient world of Assyria. For all of Manship's modernity and links to the Art Deco world, he still reveals his academic traditions in his figures. Most of his sculptures contain symbols of the ancient world as well as forms borrowed across time. Indeed, many of the sculptures of the gardens call upon mythology, history and neoclassicism for their inspiration. Two examples are the massive granite carving of *Pegasus* by Laura Gardin Fraser, set in a great pool, and Albert Wein's excessively muscular limestone work, *Phryne Before the Judges*, mounted on a plinth hidden by ground cover.

The Roman goddess Diana was a popular mythological subject for sculptors of the early twentieth century, a subject frequently chosen for the gardens of the wealthy. Among Brookgreen's six Dianas are two by Anna Hyatt Huntington and one by Augustus Saint-Gaudens. Anna's *Diana of the Chase* is set low, in conjunction with the water. Standing on a globe with her torso turned to give the sculpture a subtle counterpoise, her dog stands on his hind legs, turning against her legs. Saint-Gaudens's *Diana* stands on the ball of one foot high atop a column, a majestic yet strangely sensual work from the famous sculptor who did no other nudes. These two excellent works are for me the epitome of the elegance which characterizes the integration of the sculpture into the cultivated nature of the garden. The Huntington sculpture is almost reachable by the viewer, while the Saint-Gaudens stands high above in splendor.

Not far from the Saint-Gaudens, one comes upon the amazing *Fountain of the Muses*, a work by Carl Milles, thought by some to be his finest achievement. These eight figures in and around a pool, some atop fishes, were old friends who greeted me for over twenty-five years at the Metropolitan Museum of Art. Through the efforts of one of Brookgreen's trustees, the *Muses* came to Brookgreen, as figures in action, to spread their joy and speak of the glories of the arts that come as gifts from the gods.

Wandering in the gardens, one is struck again and again by the exquisite beauty of sculptures set in the living silence of nature. The experience defies definition; it engages the spirit in a way that cannot happen in a gallery. This feeling is especially evident in the Mary Alice and Bennett A. Brown Sculpture Court, a recent and stunning renovation of a Huntington-designed building original to the garden where pools connect the outdoor courtyard galleries.

EvAngelos Frudakis's reclining nude, resting on one leg and reaching with one arm from her stone perch, is a masterful piece in the center of one pool. Many small bronzes, such as Robert Henry Rockwell's *Survival of the Fittest*, are exceptional in their anatomy and action, while Charlotte Dunwiddie's small bronze *Toro Bravo* exhibits the grandeur of a large bull. This gallery is a splendid complement to the greater gardens, as the confined space permits many sculptures to be seen in a short span, and the close grouping allows the works to be seen and studied in conjunction with one another. In the four corners of the gallery are aluminum sculptures by Anna Hyatt Huntington, each depicting a different animal or bird group: bears, wild boars, jaguars and vultures. They are the mid-career work of the artist, an unsurpassed modeler of form who enhances surfaces with an inventive use of texture which suggests the fur or feathers of each creature.

Outside the gallery, the viewer may stumble upon another small bronze by Albert Laessle: *Duck and Turtle*, an unusual and fine composition located in an out-of-the-way spot. From this, we learn one of the most important lessons of the Huntington Sculpture Garden. Many of the outstanding works of the collection have had their sites landscaped and architecturally prepared to enhance the sculpture and to allow exceptional opportunities for viewing it from different vantage points and in different conditions of light. Yet throughout the collection, there are many sculptures installed in less commanding sites which are among the greatest works of art at Brookgreen. The viewer is delighted to find such extraordinary works as Gaston Lachaise's group of three aluminum swans facing each other as they rest on a circular form floating in a pond. Crowded by plantings and standing against a background of vine leaves is the shy, charming and sensual bronze child by Jo Davidson, *My Niece*. Marshall Fredericks is represented by several sculptures at Brookgreen, including the superb *Gazelle Fountain*, elevated so as to be silhouetted against the sky. The gazelle is surrounded by a hawk, rabbit, grouse and otter at its base. Not to be overlooked is Fredericks's stunning *Siberian Ram*, a medium-scale bronze imaginatively rendered. The distinguished medalist Gertrude Lathrop is represented by two sculptures seen only at special exhibitions because of their fragile patinas. Her *Great White Heron*, cast in Benedict nickel, and her unusually textured *Little Lamb* are charming yet strong works. These smaller sculptures can provide untold pleasures and discoveries. Brookgreen's collection of modern and contemporary animal sculptures is unequaled. Wheeler Williams's panthers, Anna Hyatt Huntington's alligators and jaguars, Beatrice Fenton's sea turtle, Albino Manca's eagle and Elie Nadelman's magnificent stag are a few. These sculptures compare admirably with works of other periods and demonstrate that this subject continues to engage the thoughts and imagination of our most creative minds.

Returning to the garden entrance, one comes to the Callie and John Rainey Sculpture Pavilion, which houses two art galleries for changing exhibitions. On the façade of one gallery is a remarkable high-relief sculpture of ocean waves, a 20-foot-long horizontal bronze by Stanley Bleifeld. Frequently on exhibition in one of the galleries are some of the collection's important early historical works, as well as some delicate sculptures which cannot withstand the elements. This gallery often adds to the cast of famous historic figures such as Daniel Chester French, Frederick MacMonnies, John Quincy Adams Ward, Hiram Powers and George Grey Barnard. Barnard's delicate and graceful single sculpture in the collection, *Maidenhood*, is a model of his skill as a marble carver. As one passes between the galleries, one is faced with the three life-sized figures of Richard Miller's *Saint James Triad*.

In a pathway through a great open field, the writer's twelve-foot high *Heron, Grouse and Loon* are intricately balanced on boulders. They point the way to Brookgreen Gardens' new E. Craig Wall, Jr. Lowcountry Center. At the entrance to the Lowcountry Center stands Anna Hyatt Huntington's *Wildlife Column*, a late work derived from earlier motifs. The animals at the base and the soaring cranes at the top are fitting symbols for Brookgreen today, which continues to acquire the best examples of figurative art being produced in America, while its educational mission expands to serve an ever-wider public.

Elliot Offner
Andrew W. Mellon Professor in the Humanities
  Emeritus, Smith College
Past President, National Sculpture Society

Arboretum

Don Quixote - Anna Hyatt Huntington and *Sancho Panza* - C. Paul Jennewein

Flying Wild Geese - Marshall Fredericks

Nature's Dance - A. Stirling Calder

Gazelle Fountain - Marshall Fredericks

Heron, Grouse and Loon - Elliot Offner

Heron, Grouse and Loon - Elliot Offner

The Thinker - Henry Clews, Jr.

Seated Woman - Leonda Finke

The Saint James Triad - Richard McDermott Miller

Cares for Her Brothers - Veryl Goodnight

Dogwood Pond

Phryne Before the Judges - Albert Wein

Joy of Motherhood - Willard Hirsch

American St. Francis - Charles Parks

Carolina Terrace

Actaeon - Paul Manship

Lioness and Cub - Hope Yandell

Forest Idyl - Albin Polášek

Diana - Paul Manship

Alligator Bender - Nathaniel Choate and *Alligator Fountain* - Anna Hyatt Huntington

Fauns at Play - Charles Keck

Joy - Karl Gruppe

Man Carving His Own Destiny - Albin Polášek

Anne's Garden

Child of Peace - Edward Fenno Hoffman III

Scratching Doe - Dan Ostermiller

Tortoise Fountain - Janet Scudder

Garden Room for Children

Sunflowers - Charles Parks

Freedom of Youth - Rosie Sandifer

Frog Baby - Edith B. Parsons

Frog Baby - Edith B. Parsons

Deerhounds Playing - Anna Hyatt Huntington

The Thinker - Marshall Fredericks

Eat More Beef - Sandy Scott

Mother and Baby Bear - Marshall Fredericks

Brown Bears - Anna Hyatt Huntington

Flute Boy - Richard Recchia

Flute Boy - Richard Recchia

Happiness - Nancy Reynolds

Little Lady of the Sea - Ernest Bruce Haswell

Center Garden

Pastoral - Edmond Amateis

Dionysus - Edward McCartan

Dogwood Garden

Riders of the Dawn - A. A. Weinman

Nereid - Berthold Nebel

Reclining Woman with Gazelle - Walter Rotan

Nereid - Berthold Nebel

Dogwood Garden

Dream - Joseph Nicolosi

Pomona - Joseph Renier

Live Oak Allée

Disarmament - Daniel Chester French

Live Oak Allée Scene

Live Oak Allée Entrance; in the distance, *Dionysus* - Edward McCartan

The Youthful Franklin - Tait McKenzie

Live Oak Allée; in the distance, *Diana of the Chase* - Anna Hyatt Huntington

Jaguar - Anna Hyatt Huntington

Fountain Garden

Neptune - Wheeler Williams

Pegasus - Laura Gardin Fraser

Pegasus - Laura Gardin Fraser

Fountain of the Muses - Carl Milles

Diana - Augustus Saint-Gaudens

Diana - Augustus Saint-Gaudens

Fountain Garden

Fountain of the Muses - Carl Milles

Old Kitchen Garden

Nymph and Fawn - C. Paul Jennewein

Peace Fountain - Sandy Scott

Palmetto Garden

Samson and the Lion - Gleb Derujinsky

Ecstasy - Gleb Derujinsky

Ecstasy - Gleb Derujinsky

Samson and the Lion - Gleb Derujinsky

Aerial of Palmetto Garden

Girl with Fish - Harriet Hyatt Mayor

Diana Garden

Lion - Anna Hyatt Huntington

Griffin - Paul Manship

Sea Urchin Garden

African Elephant - Robert Henry Rockwell

Diana by Augustus Saint-Gaudens, distant view from Sea Urchin Garden

Sea Urchin - Edward Berge and Henry Berge

The Afternoon of the Faun - Bryant Baker

Other Sculpture

Len Ganeway - Derek Wernher

Young America - Joseph Walter

Youth Taming the Wild - Anna Hyatt Huntington

Wind on the Water - Richard McDermott Miller

Brown Bears - Anna Hyatt Huntington

Fighting Stallions - Anna Hyatt Huntington

The Visionaries - Anna Hyatt Huntington

Pledge Allegiance - Glenna Goodacre

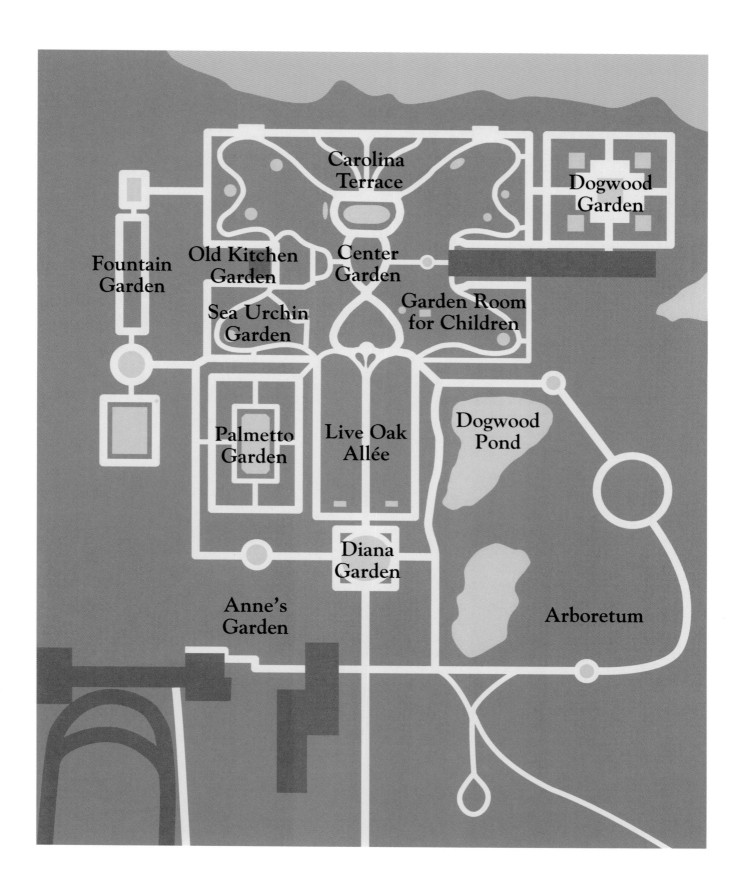

Fountain
Garden

Carolina
Terrace

Dogwood
Garden

Old Kitchen
Garden

Center
Garden

Sea Urchin
Garden

Garden Room
for Children

Palmetto
Garden

Live Oak
Allée

Dogwood
Pond

Diana
Garden

Anne's
Garden

Arboretum